rile & heave

(everything reminds me of you)

poetry by
Lindsay Illich

Texas Review Press
Huntsville, Texas

FIRST EDITION
Requests for permission to acknowledge material from the work should be sent to:

> Permissions
> Texas Review Press
> English Department
> Sam Houston State University
> Huntsville, TX 77341-2146

Poems in this collection have appeared in the following publications:

Adirondack Review, Arcadia Magazine, Bluestem Quarterly, Buddhist Poetry Review, Coachella Review, Cranky, Damselfly, Freshwater Review, Gulf Coast, Hunger Mountain, Hurricane Blues: How Katrina and Rita Ravaged a Nation, LETTERS: Journal of the Yale Divinity School, Improbable Worlds: An Anthology of Texas and Louisiana Poets, The Mom Egg, North American Review, Occupoetry, Rio Grande Review, Salamander, Sundog Lit, Texas Poetry Journal, and *Tupelo Press 30/30 Anthology.*

cover art: Iris Kumar
cover design: Nancy Parsons, Graphic Design Group

Library of Congress Cataloging-in-Publication Data

Names: Illich, Lindsay, 1977- author.
Title: Rile & heave : (everything reminds me of you) / by Lindsay Illich.
Other titles: Rile and heave
Description: First edition. | Huntsville, Texas : Texas Review Press, [2017]
   | Capitalization by the author.
Identifiers: LCCN 2016047390 (print) | LCCN 2016048217 (ebook) | ISBN
   9781680031171 (pbk.) | ISBN 9781680031188 (ebook)
Subjects: LCSH: Man-woman relationships--Poetry. | LCGFT: Experimental poetry.
Classification: LCC PS3609.L56 A6 2017 (print) | LCC PS3609.L56 (ebook) | DDC
   811/.6--dc23
LC record available at https://lccn.loc.gov/2016047390

table of contents

And how does a body break
bread with the word when the word
has broken. Again. And. Again.

C.D. Wright

Joints: whole and not whole, connected-separate,
consonant-dissonant.

Heraclitus

I became a fabulous opera.

Arthur Rimbaud

rile & heave

(everything reminds me of you)

~

The price of inertia is throated,
caustic. An apple cored,

browning up with crazy. Abrupt
the one solitude is craved.

Seams along a collar stay
and goes your meeting of green.

Even elephants could be considered
pastoral. The Lord has risen,

but I am exhausted. And as we
draw the churching of women

let us turn now to the Google
image search, the pylons,

O the modernity. Honey, the rum-filled
Australia we dreamed of

is nothing compared to the night
I entered your name

and up came the crotch shots
of the billionaire Russian émigré's girlfriend.

The world is filling up with
gladness, see. Its utterance

becomes a door. Enter.

syllabus: a delorean

Cross-legged in the grass, baring
her breast to a doll:

This is a door. This is a trowel.
Nouns make sentences.

The mimetic capacity
of Scotch tape, dead cells,

the slew of grackle
in the trumpet vine.

The apostolic concision
of catalogues: chifferobe, stamen.

Tell her to unlearn a room
and think, stanza.

heteroglossia

for T.H.M.

The birds have woken me before dawn,
in the left margin of June without you:

some loves are textual, coming paratactically,
Alexandrine, getting smoked like a Cuban.

                              And you, caesuredly.

So the morning is about to do her rise
thing, the lupines, the vireos, and I'm back

in the rivers we waded in, floated down,
discussed abstractly and mythologically

(Lovett, Char, Lethe, Charon), their uterine
beds, our brokenness, your dopkit

and mesquite (neither keeps you).
Nothing has kept you on the globe

where I learned the word *gypsum*
yesterday. How boring is the

heaven-is-a-mansion thing, esp. since
how much better would a river be

where you and me are alive
and always alive with moving.

So the birdsong—the dawn chorus—
man they sure do remind me of you,

the white-throated sparrow oppositing
death, esp. Brother, fisher, owl of awake

and sleep, some nights we got so drunk
I was afraid you would go home,

put a frozen pizza in the oven
and pass out, the house burning down

around you. And this morning's sobriety
means no you. You would have hated it.

But the summer, the short north of it,
the bird derries, the beautiful derrieres

on the ferry (otherwise a bag of marsh-
mallows), classic blues, the scissor-tail

and colic roar of a river—
even though it's highway noise—

just like when we lived together: shearing,
in love with a draft of forever, your bed

one room over, your love the adjacent
possible, a door (I get it now) opening

on a river called *help*, where no waters
overwhelm, where the soul sits, discursive,

no burning second story to pull you from,
all the dry bones crumbled like windowsill bees

reanimate, breathed into, singing back
to life the morning, calling the sun

back up, a poesis coming true, word by
word, the dark clouds lightening, lifting

droozy dawn from horizon, ceasuredly.

gulf bodies

before their faces came in
and the water rose to the gulf

your twins were gone and you were glad
they didn't live to see

you stilled with them, gathered up their coarse
blood left behind and pulled out

(women are told monstrous things
in the cool palms of stirrups) and you go

on rummaging through boxes for some-
thing worth saving: matchbooks

from Hotel Monteleone, a newspaper
clipping announcing a first engagement,

a pair of black steel binoculars
in their hard leather case (the leather

laces of the case's seams darker
than the rest of the leather)

everyday your breasts receding, back
to the shore of unmother, and you watch

the softblue light of evening news,
where a real mother has lost her

real son, and she's looking through the glass
at your belly, crying, *I want my peoples*

sea turtle

For the way the halls and viewing bays
stay dark while the great tank glows like a soul

lustrated in blue light, I applaud the aquarium
architect. From left to right the silent ones swim

in and out of sight. They move like thoughts,
like memory, like a Wes Anderson diorama

of earthly delights: lionfish, an albacore,
a fever of stingrays—and then like a wound,

a sea turtle at eye level. I recognize in hers
your thin-lipped disdain for being analyzed,

your inexorable wariness of just being.
The truth is you show up like this everywhere:

on the trail, in *New Yorker* cartoons, in my own
dark carapace where I keep all lost loves

(think of all those things you saved).
I am full of you. In and out of view,

swimming, still swimming, through pages
of blue, one after another, whole

fascicles of being bound up and buoyed,
I'm touching the plate glass, leaning

into it, in a way wanting more
but finally losing sight of you, and

having seen enough for one day
pushing off the glass like the edge

of a pool, just hard enough to keep going,
and finally (I *am* sorry) walking away.

earthsmoke & rue

even good days—
when I hear sirens

for a split second
it's carrying you

or when I don't recognize
a number on my phone,

it's someone calling to tell me
you've fallen in a river

in a dream it's you
at the bottom of the swimming pool

pls don't let it worry you
that I can't forget the Golden Gate Bridge,

its simple being there
even bad days—

I consider the possibility
that my split ends

iterate a coastline:
our warm morning sheets

no more than five cells
away from each another

double that & triple it
& by the power law vested in me

even the smallest words *en masse*
begin to form a rational structure,

the world making itself into
a single heartbeat, & even

your not being here will stop it

said the house of "You're Beautiful"

gone your brill
library of tinsel,

shock of humble
drop, Ben

your death
left me

saturated
with lightbulb

hanging
with the down

dread of incandescence

ax land

I can't remember where but maybe at the Ptarmigan
between smokes or maybe it was that time house left

(I can't remember shit these days) before him before
that boy ruined her when it was clean & lavender

& spray-tanned & lemon-streaked, her shoulder
proffered, & he pinned I watched him

pull up the morning he quit her (Daddy's words),
reach over her in the cab of his truck

yelling *get out* next to the trash barrels his truck
(Windex bottle, spit can, wilted greens,

the tobacco smell more than I could stomach)
open the passenger door (unhinge), groom

of shampooed floorboards,
as if the violence on stage wasn't happening

(*Trojan Women*, crushed oranges), like a person might
who was made to sit up straight against a tree-

trunk, trying hard to pretend not to notice his ax
land in the bark above her head to ruin her

there was a tree we found in the woods carved up
with their initials I can't remember if she said

it was a felling or splitting maul she said
it casually, as if the violence wasn't happening

apologia for mountaineering

I climbed the mountain because Stevie Nicks
made it sound so nonchalant.

I climbed the mountain because I knew the word
krummholz referred to trees

penultimate to treeline,
leafless and arthritic, barely able to sustain

love at that height. I climbed it because
orienteering meant something to you, our

topos was radiant. I climbed the thing
to be interesting, to say I did you.

I climbed the mountain so I could sign my name
with the tiny yellow golf pencil in the summit log

and sit in the wind shelter eating a pb & j
and regret wearing contact lenses because

my eyes are burning, but Jesus
you look good against Long's Peak,

the earth almost smooth down there,
me still trying to catch my breath,

relieved we're finally over.

manitoba widow flies

The last week in November
opens out in a row
of empty boxes. Blood
oranges have come into season.

You slip on the garden shoes
and step outside the screen
door, listen to the tap,
taptap close,

crack open a beer,
pour it out in a shallow
baking pan between
two rows of winter lettuce,

a leaf of which reminds
you of your own hands.
Texas for the first time
too small for your morning

grief. It opens out
in boxes and rows, its outline
of the gulf a shark bite,
the jagged edges worn

down in the crack, crash-
crash waves off the jetty,
a stretch of which reminds
you of the leaf of winter

lettuce, a leaf of which
reminds you of his hands.

being in the draft of

> *And once we, being so attracted, are drawing toward what draws us,*
> *our essential being already bears the stamp of that "draft." As we*
> *are drawing toward what withdraws, we ourselves point toward it. We*
> *are who we are by pointing in that direction—not unlike an inci-*
> *dental adjunct but as follows: this "being in the draft of" is in itself*
> *an essential and therefore constant pointing toward what withdraws.*
> *To say "being in the draft of" is to say "pointing toward what with-*
> *draws."*   Martin Heidegger, "What Calls for Thinking?"

It was hers I knew best: walk-in,
pink felt cowgirl hat, a dialed radio,
red slicker with matching hat and black
rubber boots size six-and-a-half,
a Kelly green attaché she used
to cart around marked-up essays.
To darn, and bolero, a turquoise amulet,
a shag skirt from an Iranian student.
No outfits but in things. Then there was
the Rubaiyat, a wooden case with a glass
compass inside, an early model Kodak
with a cube flash, cassette tapes, a slide
machine and boxes of slide, stacks
of catalogs with marked pages,
a commemorative Ronald Reagan plate.

There are the same number of bones
in a giraffe's neck as there are in the human one:
seven. She often told this joke about scrod,
how she never heard its past perfect form,
which no one ever really got. Like the way
she pronounced *Don Juan* according to Byron,
and when she met anyone openly gay she
stammered on about the Gay Cavaliers.
She would come and go, correcting
my pronunciation of *Michelangelo*.
In accordance to her personal objective
correlative, her legs when she was old
became storkish, wearing even capris
cuffed (I could only conclude) to show

how her body at the end was becoming
poem, a word she said reverently, the *oe*
in her mouth a single vowel.

The only thing that works now (between us)
are nursery rhymes. When she was good
she was very very good. It's the only
thing she remembers. I have her master's
thesis, "Social Concepts in the Drama of Elmer Rice,"
which I haven't read. There is a light.
There are scissors. She becomes
a babe in the woods again.

In the closet I found a photograph taken
maybe 1940 or so—def before the war—
she is posing in a bathing suit, hand on hip.
And pages of handwritten notes on the backs
of purple mimeographed grammar exercises
about my grandfather's not loving her
the way she wanted to be loved. Her loneliness.
Her blindness. At first it was small noticings:
the cabinets were dirty, the cabbage in the slaw
brown, the sugar ants patrolling her kitchen.
Some days if the weather held, she picked up
sticks in the yard. Even her makeup was mawkish.

She read me Wordsworth's "Michael"
when I was too young for it. She spoiled
me with new clothes. There was a song
she sang about two orphans on the steps
of a church I can't remember the name of,
the onus of tragedy like starch in her pillowcases.
The relatives laughed at her salmon pâté,
and I never got it, that or what happened
between her and God, because I could feel
the enmity, the sadness in her feral white
hair. If it could just be about the Word
and if she could let it be about the Word
being with God in the beginning
then maybe she would be comforted.

afternoon

Under you, an opportunity.
Maybe wings. Something sparrow-
like and rood. It's the terrible

trick you play with your hands
deseeding an avocado—
slamming in, then a turn.

In shades, the touch.
Kindness a kind of beam
you light up the dark insides

of my body with. Light
as a gesture. Countenance
as lift and blade.

I don't need to be under you
to feel it.

snowbound: an american idyll

For Ben Lerner

Al Roker, star-spangled—give me your mesoscale
bands, isotherms not mutability, say the future
so I'll know it. Desire is recognition, a kind

of thinking, the ends of time
a door on one side marked *free will* and
on the other *predestination*. I walked into

the future, and mine was a room: bleach
white plaster, birch branches in the vaulting.
My limbs tried to be owls. Put your hands

together. If I wanted to be outside well
then I would be, but someone here thought
put your hands together. Standing at the window,

looking through its falling, consider its legibility:
a cardinal sliced the distance between me
and the fencepost. What if my whole life

is a series of innocences. The geese are a series
of innocences coming down from Canada.
In Buffalo, where pink sky and listen

little boy with the delicious potato chips
like suns, eating them like suns:
winter is a minor baptism, Peter

is this your annotated bibliography, your
help, I suppose. It was the rain gave us
imagination to invent a heaven, sky

so big we thought about it all
the time, the weather or not central
to our understanding of what it is

to be human. I look at you and I can't
think of anything. All day the nothing falling
on the heaps of nothing, to the wheel-

ridge and then the sills, nothing coming
from nothing, Al Roker standing
in the nothing falling, the houses

sinking in the nothingness, night
falling in nothingness and quietude,
the first alone the angels did say.

december 30

I've written you plotting & plodding,
sweet one. I say this is now.

You are key, lock, bed clothes
pulled off. I am a register

you sing in. How is it love's
consequence can be so light?

I've written you sundry & careless,
a catapult of windchime.

I sometimes think of us as forgetful
& only remembering each other

like claustrophobes wanting the dense
space of football fields, the silver-scaled

seats of empty stadium. Or deep
in the night's sorrow, when you hear me

breathing, we are one
continent. You found a scrap of paper

with Cormac McCarthy #5
scrawled on it & wondered what I meant,

& you want to get it
so bad. You want Cormac McCarthy #5

to mean something
prayerlike & migratory,

falling like a Leonid, but
it doesn't mean anything.

I imagine sewing it
in my hem, published

inconsequentially,
as love sometimes is.

anatomy lessons

That you thought china bones
existed only in the bodies of dolls—
that's one. Ligature for elegy.

The body of you and this body.
The body of you and other bodies.
The body of you making bodies

of all bodies. A leg crooked
over your hip. Tonight, clavicle.
Tonight, sweet tendon. Tonight

the chuffing away degrees
of separation. That you thought
a body permeable, soluble

as salt, that this body could
matter after that body didn't—
that's two. We are sealed.

Hermetic as walnuts.
A cast of bodies lying in dust
along the smooth edge

of headboard, along
the winter curve of wrist.
That you thought your body

Godlike, plunging your hands
in its dust and making of it
another body—that's three.

calendary

Low as the heart's low
thrum, dark as moon wink.

Recall the piano bench,
a door jamb, losing
all taste for living here.

The little house in a row
of little houses forgets to mean.

A slow middle life of books
& paperclip, a diaper's
heavy weight, the dog's bowl
always empty again.

The dirty dish, dull.
A dram of aspirin, hum
of appliance, awl. Winterness,
carved carbuncle of January.

Some splinter errata, a misspelling,
and then waking up again,
kneeling at the coffeemaker,
bargaining with what gods will listen.

ENGLAND

She opened the door and found him on the floor, face down on the carpet, spread eagle. It was the position and not the time of day that disturbed her. To be on the floor is sometimes comfortable, the way the hard cold tile feels good on your face sometimes, but this was a man who appeared at once to be drawn from imaginary cords from the four corners of the room and to be showing what the body would do at the moment of explosion. She was wrong about both. He was making himself abject. Open at all the private parts and love so low to the ground, low as he could possibly go. It was the position of arrest. It's a door she can't close.

white room dendrology

When I arrived
you had lost almost everything—
your black wristwatch, both rings, the knowledge
of swallowing. In the white room
all there's left to do here
is die. Amen and amen.

The doctor arrives
with pictures of your heart
in his coat pocket. He draws
them out like folded money,
shows me the black and white
branching veins of the ventricle.

And the weeks after arrive like
the picture of your heart in my back
pocket. I come and go,
Montaigne in the purple sage.
I come and go and you
remain in the monosyllable, a sheet

tucked under your dead arm, your
twig legs kick back
the covers. You cough, and I
look in your eyes for the almost
contralto in the cough. The good
arm reaches for my hands. You
look at my wristwatch, my rings.

Yesterday was the same
losing and penance. Amen and amen.
You sway in and out, mostly out
and almost gone, and almost,
almost losing everything—
the steady wind through your chest
my fingers growing out and budding
the roots burrowing through the bed
the floor the foundation and soon
sycamore amen and amen and
all there's left to do is die.

what the f dear mister Chrysler

(with thanks to Sugar)

right there with the big nasty contrails
of disaster behind me and

the loved the left the gone and
even Lord remember the shuttle

blowing up right there in front of us and
fireweed & anklebones and my

sweet son somewhere in the blue
and all of it right there bearing down

hard and not even knowing
where it was I was

going in the middle of
what have I done, the sidewalk

furious with people
right there on 42nd where Bryant Park

ends and the Public Library
begins, right there, I looked up.

I looked up and everything stilled:
the f was my life

and I was answering it

first words

As if his voice searched the world over
for a word, the smallest conceived,
and when he found it,

his voice pressed it between his thumb
and forefinger to make it smaller
still, so small it became a tiny

pebble he tossed in the shoreline
of his mouth. He is tasting
his first word's salt, its lightness

and strum. He is hearing
the first word shape into shelves
of continents, a word never

uttered the world over. It
is his. It is mine. It
is the first day and night

dawning on his tongue, the world's
blue luminosity humming
the first chord of creation,

a world just now set in fierce
motion. It is ours. It is ours.

fear & trembling

I'll tell you a story
because I've had it with your asking,

is every day the same?
or, how much does an iPad cost?

Once upon a time there was your smooth shark
nose rubbing up on my face. There is your

lifting my shirt
like a stage curtain to see

how fat I've grown.
Hell is paved with allegory.

And so,
A rat tells a hedgehog,

once I was digging out front
and found a metal bookmark

that said when you reach for the stars
you don't have far to fall,

and I thought what hogwash
especially since I found it in the dirt.

But what I did was clean it up
and that night when I had read

all I wanted to read, I put the bookmark
in the book's gutter where it fit

nicely and did its work in the world.
And then, and then, and then

goes the gold from gossamer wings
and I will not advise you to major

in the liberal arts, but I'll tell you what—
there was a time it made sense to do so.

summer

Go make of me
a walrus head.
Circumnavigate

a set of sheets.
Lock out the lazy.
Do with me

what you would
an elephant hide.
Snap peas.

Be little girl in diapers
pressing her bare
feet into the crawling

thyme. Memorize
me, my late
darkness. Do with me

a dance to plunder the winter
tune, the damp
colic, the dream

cloven. Summer lies
back, counting
her fingers

over & over.
She waits
for us to get tired

of her madness, waits
for us to sunburn & wish
her heat would break.

15 Seconds (My Vagina Is Opening Like a Flower)

How long a moon long, the dodge of out,
this pushing from the oh-fix-me living right.

O Lord. A year. A paraphrase. O delish.
O sentimental argument, Lord.

The long moon, the grass growing,
tip and strive. We find love

when we're cowards, dots
on one end of a text message,

typing, bores of syntax.
Dear Lord, your liminality

is dotted, elliptical like the sense
of now (dot dot dot), 15 seconds long

long moon (pls Lord help me).

in situ

Somewhere in deepness
you're digging in

beat, oh beat, Deepness
keep o heart turn,

matter-of-factly, in the style
of dove flight *beginning*

where our bodies of argument
lay head to foot, our deep

coterie of insights, Deepness,
about your unleaving

me, leavening me, your
body a brief cartel of breaking

this water breaking

LEL

It takes a very small house
to teach you the language of house.

In the language of house
we learned interiority, its way

of shade and nook and abode.
In "house" children pray

to the grosgrain gods for bead
molding, for high-backed chairs

and chifferobes with fluted legs.
Windows for eyes, a saltbox profile,

a house where we could work it out:
a theory of wainscotting,

the intricate psychology of parquet,
how good an eave feels

against yr forehead. Before
a house and before a builder,

before survey before a before
any of us were here

there were bones. We remember
the rafters of her ribs, the warm

furnace of her belly grates, even
her teeth were there for us.

It took a small house, sister.

great comet of 1680 (ISON)

It sounds messed up
but in the end I imagine

making paper maché
globes covered with our faces

& hanging them from the ceiling,
minus everything we thought it was

we were doing here (that is,
telos): the room will be full of us

What a firework in the sky
it would be when we died,

what a flash of seahorse head

F train

ur lush & clean
even automatically

even cool like chrome
handrails, ur hand

next to mine, laughter
among ur bracelets

& there is

O windless inside
O skin keeping the blood in

rinsing the coral piece under the faucet, I became

Bone done, sustainability
the enemy of interesting.

The secret of bare is being
prudently arrested, dis-

possession: sweet 'n low,
octave strewn sofa, simple

treedom. I went to the woods
as I went to Carlsbad:

alone, hoping not to be
disappointed. I went thirsty

even though I lived in water.
I wanted to travel the world

minus Asia. I wanted your
finger in my mouth, urspice.

I went to the living room
for celebrity, for heaven laid

news on your phone, a glimpse
of how other people live.

<to be honest>

I want to make you the best
sandwiches of your life

I want to remind you:
nothing in this book

is more beautiful than
the big snow just turned from rain

Everything is through it
Everything is just Every second

a thousand fevers of dash
streaming from the up there

And even when it isn't snowing
it's you calling from

nothing falling I'm calling
you in the nothing falling

esperanza, very house

the house we worry
what to do in

is the same house
we go in & out of

the same house
that lives with our
alternative sincerity

the house that breathes
in exhaust, wren song,
surfeit, danger

the house is scuse me
scuse me mellow wood

that we wouldn't trade
for the most beautiful
Taco Bell in the world

(the one we passed
in Half Moon Bay)

this is the house
bruise, the house rule

the very house
we worry what to do in

geography lessons

When the glacier scraped over
the Manhattan schist—

see the grainline—when the long
time it took, before the husk,

before the planes before the dusk
before the night before the night,

when the glacier moved these
lines got made, and these,

grooves and striations, moraines
and have nots.

It took
a long time. A long, long time.

Then the middle part of life
washes in. Then erratics, then emails

for "help, I suppose," appointments,
deletions, the offices of gray alphabets,

another meeting, another meeting,
and another meeting comes to mind.

We are always awake. At least it feels
that way.

At night, the states are just states,
the world just a world, and we're in a room,

dreaming of falling asleep together, of
breathing the same air,

we are dreaming of being together even though
the world feels ruinous and strange.

In the morning, walking
the edge of the grass

where snow is receding, the daffodils
shooting, the tiny buds on the pink bush just

getting ready to push. In a few weeks,
it will be all pink and white, pink and white,

the curbs
mottled with pink and white.

We look up
and see birds in the seamless sky.

I tell her
the world was hewn with grapevine,

counsel, and eruption, cut
on the bias,

and that's how lines are made
and we are made and how

the mind comes to the edge of itself
and looks out from a continental shelf

but way down under all of it
we're the same stuff as the stuff way over there

and yes it took a long time, but a long time
is sometimes what it takes

for love to sink in.

frozen bees

I wanted the bees to die
& meanly, for having broken
in the house. I did it
with hairspray, freezing
their wings midair. And they fell
stunned, scattered across the hard-
wood. Cereal-like.

You asked *do you think bees
have a word for everything?*

You mean like a word for stiff
wing, the stuff they fell through
before hitting the floor?

Yes. No.

You boarded a train.
I swept up the dead
bees. Wondered at the word
austere. I don't know
where to put the bed
anymore. Wonder if there's

a love so unofficial
it can't be spoken, words
having frozen in the presence of it.

cleaning house

Sister, it's just about done
and we're in the clear, safe

in the day's margin. Make me
one of those bourbon drinks

with a quarter key lime
and let's perch here awhile.

There's nothing left to be cleaned
and everyone left to be loved

but for once let's not think
about how we're supposed

to look at this age. Sister,
we've grown into each other

like the limbs of those
trees and from here I don't

know whose branch this
or nest that. And underground

I bet our cursive roots
are winding through each other.

So this is what one mind
looks like. And there you

go again blinking like a cursor
and in blows these words

and after, Sister, the sound
of your broom, sweeping.

where the joyful anything: please spring

God likes a good sentence
just as much as I do:

inviolate, his nomenclatures
seize the daisy.

On quiet afternoons
when the snow stops

and all the still woods
still, his x finds

its way in the crawl space,
runs along the turret.

O hear his scratch
inside us, still.

anklebones & cups

among the chrysalis even
the scarves you sometimes

fall asleep in, a galaxy nebula
who spent the last million

million years calling out
take my picture

what he did with the moon tonight

What he did with the moon
tonight was he
pressed her through a sieve,
& out came the blazoned
bones scattering
across the floor of sky.
What he didn't count on
was the unintended consequence
of losing her light, the stars
coupling, their penurious
leaning into each other's
gravity, burning up
with the need to shine.

on watching you eat a clementine

Your mouth tends the pith
with such sweet patience it

makes me want to give you
the valentine of my body scan,

a skiagraphy of bone and tendon
I watch you peel it,

can't help but think of the rind
a signature, your coffee

spoon's bravura, the aver
of morning so still it writes

itself, like the typewriter bird
whose tree outside becomes

a conference of birds, the clearing
welter of your throat, organs

on paper, my ilium
unfolding in your patient hands.

poetry

I don't suffer
from it

though sometimes
it's unreasonable

to think about
the brightness

the why turns
the owl song

congruent with
opportune to

a bellow
from the train-

yard who
would call

a train
a palindrome who

who would give
a damn

the same
coming & going

yet I do

broken down West Texas

To love someone in spite of yourself
is driving down the same road
every day without knowing
where you're going. Red light.
Green light. Gas. First
gear is temperamental.

The truck chuckles at your
nervousness. The gas gauge
falls asleep. The only letter
your hand can trace is the letter
H, and the nothing
you had in your head
spills out a little each mile.
Your windshield stares back
as if to say *I'll show you*
what I want to show you.

You drive until the tires
can't hold a penny, and
the heads of mountains
fall off—
            you're sixty miles
from Junction.

Caution crosswinds and
one hundred seventeen
windmills. The sun
doesn't go down
so much as the mesa
sucks it out of the sky.

At night, you are left
to be redeemed, in spite
of yourself—
            the truck a skin
            you can't climb out of.
The signs are all the same.

reams of grass

Father the inkjet, mother the laser,
a daughter for a printer's tray.

The alphabet of being
come apart letter by letter

until the universe impressed
a very large door on her belly

out of whom poured the elegant:
the word, and the word was good.

And she let there. And it lived,
utterly, delightfully, within

and spine broken, birthmark
and colophon bright as eyes

lined with exclamation points.
Let there be delight,

and I feel young and amazing.
Copy fair, copy right with the world

and double space and oh
the dour of leading.

creation story

Writers are born far, far away from everyone else. Imagine a girl in an isolette on an island, nothing but banana trees around her. She grows. She eats bananas. She learns that she can weave strips of bark together to make slats then weave the slats together to make a roof to cover her nest at night when it storms. On clear nights, before she falls asleep, she would look up at the stars and moon and have no idea that once someone was up there, looking back at little blue Earth. She would say goodnight to the sky, heave her roof over her nest and sleep. One morning, she got up to go wash her face in the spring that met the shore. She knelt down and scooped the water in her hands and lapped it on her face—two, three, four times. She dried her eyes with her dress hem, and when she opened them she saw a paper boat floating by in the stream. She got up and walked with it as it floated, then faster it went and she followed. Then, running out into the water before she lost sight of it, she reached and swam and swam harder until yes, she got it. Back at the shore, breathless, she held it up to the light. She could see that on the other side of the paper were patterns like the shapes of insects, some like bananas, dots and lines. All day she looked at them. She was certain they meant something. As the evening shade drew, she understood they were words. She recognized sun, moon, water. She touched the word moon. She read the word I. She understood you. She knew she wasn't alone. The next morning, she ironed together bits of lace and turquoise, determined to write back. She wanted to say thank you. She wanted to say you saved my life. She folded her blue lace letter into a bird and tried to make it go upstream, where the boat came from. She thought and thought and thought but couldn't make it go back. The sun was very bright, and her skin was burning. She began to wonder if she was the only one who was alone and thought, there must be millions. She made a new lace bird and on it she wrote something new: I know you think you're alone. I thought that, too. But we're in this together. The stars are beautiful, and the moon makes even the darkest nights okay. She put the bird in the water where the stream met the shore and watched it go out to sea, higher and then higher on the horizon, flying out to the next lonely islander, barely alive, until one morning when he went to the water to drink and he rose with the bird in his hand, and unfolded it, and found the words and drank again.

the universe of discourse

Sentience as
sentence

Apropos as
prose

I am as
iamb

syntax

At the table of agreements
and disagreements, we get along

with implicature, trace
eveningness through schemata,

shore and listen to these, those,
that deictic center that gets

me going when you say *hegemony,*
subvert, beyond the scope of this

We learn epitaphios, the ecstasy
of difference: lips, hands,

teeth, what it means to be
erred and human and get it

down deep, time yes
for utterance, for quiet

moments when humans related recognize their familiness

As children we don't know it any other way but as it's always been: you belong to them and they belong to you same as the roof does. But as you get older and meet new ones, and invite each other to live under another roof together, it's harder to feel belonged. Even if it's good, there's a sense that you don't quite fit. But you do watch the same shows. Then maybe babies. An ark. Plush animals. Chalkboard paint. I wish it didn't take so much time to get used to each other. One more baby. One morning you wake and think, where did I put my life. You remember one Sunday years ago when the first one was maybe three and the three of you were at the breakfast counter, you were standing, and I think the kid was on a stool. And for a flash I saw us as someone else would. I felt our pulses for a beat fall in line, an axis drawing straight down the middle of us. That was the year the oleanders had to be ripped out because we found out they were poisonous to the dog. One night I was crying and you told me to go write a poem. But then the Charles, the afternoon I was pregnant and we rented a boat, the three of us, the sailboats, the river molten with our giving over to each other. On water, we have to believe we belong to each other. The boat relaxed us. When the new baby came it was all over again. Alliance and insecurities. We told on each other. We exaggerated. One night, it was simple: tacos, we were all tired. The roof was quiet. As far as we could tell, we didn't have any leaks. He cleared the dishes and I changed the baby. I drew a bath for the boy and supervised his brushing. He tucked her in and I tucked him in, and even the big kids, we went straight to bed. I was lying there with my eyes closed listening to us breathing under our tiny roof, time making a family out of separate hearts. I want to do this well. I want to love the roof for keeping us.

samizdat

You copy me & I copy you
and we live together
wrinkle in the same dancedare

I would give you a heart-shaped
jellyfish if it were mine to give
or plagiarize a house

I would learn to love your felicity
your fair copy your affinity
for dirty marginalia

Winters would be for binding,
awls & thread & our bed
full of books where we make more books

then fly over the city in a helicopter
to drop our poems & even with
noise-reducing headphones I hear you

stomping around my heart
mumbling about the winepress becoming
a maker of leaves, all the poetry in the world

a fine mimeograph, having given itself
over to purple, your fine feet
at full stop. Here.

rustication

Tonight, I immolate
my love (my love) for you—

for ur shatoosh is
one of the world's finest—

ur
emphatic understanding
of lost thoughts
and whateverthefuckIam

ur
identical or even better
replacement body parts

which is to say
the underlying assumption
of love is ridicularity

hilarity and Iwanttokillmyself

night feet

Let it be in the twilight,
after the day's low drum of inertia
has almost knocked you over, love—

Let it be like the smooth
bed of the Em Dash—

Let it be a field of rest
for your untidy feet, the luck
named spondee, good

night.

(i)

There is no need
for prayer

when the
who is there

never leaves you

ago

Someone Thursday said,
some people raise their voices to be heard,

other people lower
their voices to be heard

You lower your voice
to the point no one can hear you

No one can hear you, not even
the absent ago, yet the words go

alive, flown from a shelf of birds,
and even then the words,

the billowbirds keep coming
alive, the words among the restive nothing

that wasn't even living a moment ago
and you know that lovely precarity

that almost kept them from kneeling down
from your lowered voice, among

the short lectures you're composing
into the hole future you're falling into

even while you're falling
in love with the hole future

falling in love with the idea
of knowing when it is the ago,

the ago will hit you
like the first words of a poem

and you'll say, Oh—
I get it. So this is death.

aperture stop

Far the focus of your
fair isosceles Your

elbow hotelness
O dear shutter O speed

My open
Click it goes

Surreptitiously
All is gone All entropy

All gemming
This our motile

universe
Outlasting even

the
outlandish coverlet

owls

atiscosa

When we bowed up to each other
I was afraid

I wore you out
the same way that caliche

has wore me out. I'm sure
on somebody's place

they have a pivot road
where they go to repent.

There's plenty more
to do around here, plenty

seguro, y claro que si.
We can pretend to be

boat people but that ain't
the honest truth. We're

hog-tied to this dirt.
Smack-dabbed, goll-durned,

like the damned Karankawas
said it was. Calf-cradled.

We surely to goodness are
calf-cradled. Like you are

to me and nothin' done
wore out between us.

before Google

Old men sat around and postulated
the pronunciation of quinoa and dour,
for starters.

Old loves were put away
and forgotten, if not easily then
at least with a sense of permanence:

leaving meant more
when there was no digital face to look at
deep in the dark when regret

autocompletes. The world seemed
almost terrible in its might-ness
but boy could we bullshit,

and the dictionary was a spellbook,
and then there was our own
dear selves, ungoogled,

protean and clean even in old age
when the only records of us
were burnable, the face of the earth

possibly wiped clean of our dust
to dust, whole nights blacked out
without the fear of pictures

turning up, the humiliation of being
there without remembering
anything. Yet. Maybe. Once upon a time

there was a mood called subjunctive
where we lived, if not blissfully
then simply, without explanation.

Nights were for plotting
and filling up a room's minutes
with our childish prayers

to please-don't-let-him-die
or mine when I cupped my hands together,
like a butterfly was inside,

pretending the Lord was there,
my breathing him in more enormous
than that old search bar's emptiness,

getting filled up with worry.
Yet. Maybe there's a kind of God
reading the catalog of our sympathies.

Who among us hasn't cleared
the cache of our search histories
out of sheer embarrassment.

I like to think of him as being online,
and I wonder if those people who dream up
marketing schemes were thinking

of a kind of God when they dreamed up the cloud,
an archivist keeping up with all
our pictures, caring about the ephemera

even we can't keep up with, grains
of sand back in the day. We go to him,
and he's backing up our drafts,

saving versions of us we don't even know
we need. What is this called
if not redemption.

say it back

To the God of wallpaper
and gold filigree—

To the great God of Kimye,
Rimbaud and washing machine—

God the giver of sleep
and single stream recycling—

God Who says Iloveyou
in the very elegant code
that downloads the latest
issue of the New Yorker—

How do we mention you
without sleeves of embarrassment,
hearts on them

omg like a girl who got sunburned
after filling an empty Suave bottle
with Mazola and basting

her big white thighs with oil,
coating every inch of them,
laying out on the driveway
until braised and blistered

How embarrassing
(come on
every good girl
deserves a Jesus)

God, we don't know how else
but to hash it out online while POTUS speaks

To like everything our mothers
post, a nod to inspired living

God we're trying to say it back
despite how it looks

Look at the air
Look how full of our voices
the stratosphere, all of us

sending up our words, our
pics, our lustrous links to stuff,
bowed, typing incessantly

rile & heave

to see things in terms of other things
is part of the deal I'm afraid

some days we can hold it at bay
and others are mournings of themselves,

the trains passing, the vertical orientation
of forest & city, a shelf of book-

titles running down spines
every thing a thing & homesick

which sounds like something
so obvious it isn't worth noting

forgive me for asking forgiveness
for being forward when we're in bed

for taking so long to put two & two
together about words & things

the rile & heave I sing when I can sing
the heart's systole & diastole

the iamb & the I am & the two & two
the breath & word the song of echocardiograms

& the world lit up in green, one foot in front
of the other, the home of poem

rushing in & out of our lungs.

CPSIA information can be obtained
at www.ICGtesting.com
Printed in the USA
LVOW08s0600230317
528145LV00004BA/8/P